The
MILLIONAIRE
SAFETY
SECRET

Escape Losses, Secure Lifelong Gains, Achieve Complete Peace of Mind, And Give Without End

Brian Lund

www.MillionaireSafetySecret.com

The Millionaire Safety Secret
Escape Losses, Secure Lifelong Gains, Achieve Complete Financial Peace of Mind, and Give Without End

By Brian Lund
Copyright © 2014, Brian Lund

ISBN: 978-1-312-24672-0

For Robyn, Hayden, Teagan and Dallin.

You are my support, my foundation, my life.
To see you have true and lasting happiness is my greatest desire.
Without your patience, love, and faith in me, this book wouldn't
have been possible. May you pursue your dreams in courage,
concern yourself with the well-being of others, and let God direct
your path in all you do.
I love you so very much!

CONTENTS

Preface
Action Today Leads To A Better Tomorrow For Yourself And Those Around You

Part One - The Perils We Face

Part Two - Fortunately, There Is Some Good News

Part Three - It's Now Time To Act!

Afterword
Give Without End

Acknowledgements

I'd like to thank the families, corporate executives, professionals, business owners and other individuals that are my clients. Thank you for encouraging me to write this book and for helping me share the timely message that is included in these pages.

I'd also like to thank all my mentors, coaches, colleagues and others in the financial services community that I've had the great pleasure of associating with, learning from, and teaching. It continually amazes me to see how many talented, smart and incredible people that surround me. I'm inspired by your passion for helping others.

To the stalwart and talented team behind me. Thank you for your faith, support, consistency and encouragement. This book wouldn't have made it to press without your help.

Lastly, to my wife, who puts up with my early mornings, late nights and busy work schedule. The work you do within the walls of our home is infinitely harder and more important than anything I could do or accomplish in the business world. Thank you for being the beautiful person you are and for nurturing and mothering our three amazing children.

Preface

Action Today Leads to A Better Tomorrow For Yourself and Those Around You

One of the reasons you're reading this book probably has a lot to do with the fact that there are people in your life who you care about. It's likely you have a family, a spouse, children, or grandchildren that look to you as an example on how to live a successful life. Maybe friends or people close to you that you consider family. Whatever the case, you're likely reading this with the goal of being in a financial position to make the most positive impact possible for your own life and in the lives of those you care about... right now and in the future.

With all the turmoil that's happening around us, there's good reason to have this goal. After seeing what's happened to financial markets over the last 15 years, the reckless way in which our government has handled the finances of this country, and countless peers, neighbors and family that have had to continue working into the time when they had originally planned to retire or slow down; it's likely you've likely taken the responsibility for your own finances and retirement into your own hands. You know that if YOU don't act, you'll be acted upon and if you don't work your own plan, you'll be subject to someone else's plan.

I applaud you. I applaud your efforts. I applaud the fact that you're taking action to ensure your future and that you're not going to sit back and watch things happen. I applaud your desires and willingness to make things happen for yourself and your loved ones. It's for you that this book is written. It's for you that aren't okay with not having control of what happens to your money, that aren't okay with watching your money dwindle and rebound every few years just to be back where you were when you started, that aren't okay with big government, or big brother watching over and ripping the rug out from under your feet right when you start to feel like you're getting a handle on things. It's for you that are open to a better way, for you that are curious, and concerned about how fees are eating into your retirement account and looking for answers on how to remedy this. This book is written for you who are willing to do the planning it takes to beat inflation and have more than enough money to last the rest of your life, that don't want to be forced to keep working well into your advanced years or have to come out of retirement and back into the workforce late in life.

There are serious bullet wounds in today's financial world that are bleeding our personal and family finances. These wounds can't be healed with band aids. To correct problems, we have to go right down to the core of the issues. Depending on someone's situation, there may have to be just a few tweaks to get on the right track, other times, some fundamental changes in mindset have to be made in order to heal the wounds.

With this, I ask you to continue with your open mindedness. I ask that you consider a few things that you may have believed that might not be entirely correct. Ask yourself these questions, "What if the majority of information that is taught in popular media about investing in the stock market and that is now considered education and gospel truth was bought and paid for by the very institutions that stand to profit off your money?" "What if traditional approaches in the market, however many stop losses and tools in place to hedge against loss, actually acted to make your life more stressful and difficult than need be?" "What if investing, in the traditional sense, was entirely the wrong thing to be doing?"

This is an intense premise, even one that could change your investing life: But these times, with the conditions we're facing today and the perils we're up against, require something different and better than what you may have done previously. If we can start with this premise, you'll have your eyes opened to some incredible knowledge and understanding. Information that will change your life for the best and those of your future generations for years to come. Information you'll hopefully want to share as part of your legacy.

So take out a pen and notepad and record a few ideas that come by reading these pages. See where you can make some changes for the better. By understanding some of these concepts, see if you can better prepare yourself and those you care about for the road ahead.

Part One

THE PERILS WE FACE

Chapter 1

An Awakening Event That Led To Massive Action

"There is a vitality, a life force, an energy, a quickening, that is translated through you into action..."
- Martha Graham

"...and action is the foundational key to all success."
- Pablo Picasso

I'll never forget the conversation I had with Nancy. Even after working with hundreds and hundreds of people on their financial strategy. This conversation sticks out significantly because of the emotion with which she spoke. It was just a phone conversation, but her message came through loud and clear. This single conversation deepened my belief in something I already knew to be true and made such an impression on me that I vowed that day to help as many people as possible understand the message she relayed. It ignited a fire in me that still burns white hot today, even after many years. It was a wakeup call for me to take massive action. I listened intently as she unraveled the story.

THE UNWANTED PHONE CALL

"We were both 65 and I remember very vividly." She said, *"We're at the Pennsylvania Zoo enjoying some much needed down time. This was our weekend escape and we were free from the worries of our rigorous daily work routines. Work was always pretty stressful and it seemed like we never really had much time together, so this weekend getaway was supposed to be a nice break."*

"We were looking at the turtle exhibit when my husband got a phone call. As he answered the call, I wondered to myself who it might it be on the other end. For some reason, my gut had a bit of a sinking feeling, thinking it may have had something to do with work, or some other bad news."

"Within the first ten seconds of him talking to this person, I could immediately tell that something was wrong. He started to look down at the ground and touch his forehead with this other hand. I was very curious as to what might be going on.

"I approached him and touched his side but he whisked away and started walking the other direction. Now I was really concerned. He put his hand on the rail and kept his head down. This time as I approached, he looked extremely pale, almost as if he was about

2

to pass out. Somewhat forcefully, I grabbed his arm and led him over to a bench."

"There we sat on this bench. Hunched over, he put his head in his hands. The pit in my stomach just got deeper and deeper. Finally, I got a glimpse into what this conversation might be about." He said to the person, 'Edward, what happened to just wait it out? I'm supposed to retire this year. I honestly don't know how to respond right now.' Then, with a few courtesies he ended the phone call."

"After he ended the call, he slowly turned to me, hesitated and then in a broken voice said, 'That was our stock market adviser. Over the last eighteen months, we've lost 45 percent.' With that admission, he hunched over again and put his head in his hands."

"I honestly didn't know how to respond either. I wanted to cry, but for some reason, I just couldn't. Looking back on it, I think I experienced some symptoms of shock."

"Thoughts just rushed through my mind, hindsight was crystal clear, the writing had been on the wall for some time. The markets had been at all-time highs just a year and a half earlier. I had read the news and knew what was going on, but hearing this and how it was affecting us personally was almost too much for me to bear."

"Pretty quickly, my shock turned to anger. Here we had been working since we were 25 years old, and even though it wasn't much in those early days, we still managed to sacrifice a small percentage of our income and squirrel it away in our stock market accounts. As a young family, that was hard to do, especially when our kids could have used some new clothes, or a new pair of shoes. My thoughts almost immediately turned to them. How would this affect the legacy we were planning on leaving to them? Thinking about all these sacrifices we had to make to save this money and how it affected the kids made me fiery mad."

"As we got older, it became easier to save money for ourselves, but we still sacrificed a great deal to be able to do that. When all our friends were buying nicer cars, and bigger homes and upgrading their lifestyle, we chose not to follow suit, all so we could save more for our eventual retirement. Honestly, it was a little hard to watch them enjoy all these nicer things in life, while we were scrimping, saving and sacrificing. But our vision was that it would all be worth it one day. <u>All of this… for nothing.</u>"

"We wanted to travel, take road trips, see Europe and the Bahamas, rent an RV or even purchase one if we liked it enough. We wanted another place to stay that was warm during the winter months. We wanted to pursue the activities and hobbies we had always dreamt of."

"We wanted to finally live as we had envisioned. But most of all, and this is what really affected me... we wanted to spend time with

4

our children, grandchildren and great-grandchildren as much as possible. We wanted to be able to do plenty of nice things for them and be there for them if they ever needed us."

"We had worked so hard for so long, we meticulously planned, scrimped, saved and sacrificed for 40 years. Then to see half of that get dashed away in a matter of 18 months was almost too much for me to handle. It felt as though the dreams that were finally almost a reality were slipping through our fingers."

"At the high point, just a short year and a half earlier, we were at almost a million dollars. I didn't even want to open our statements now, knowing they were hovering right around $500k. We had hit the $500k range almost 15 years ago, and to be back down to that level made me just want to give up. What's more, is that we had gone through this same scenario just 8 years previous. In 2001 our accounts got hammered, and here we were, right back where we started, only this time we were 8 years older and that much closer to retirement. We had been aggressively contributing for the last 8 years to try and catch up. All that money we contributed, in effect, was gone."

"What's really sad, is that money doesn't just disappear. It's always changing hands, and going somewhere. I have a few opinions on where all that money went in 2008, but people would look at me as if I were crazy if I told them my opinions. I couldn't keep thinking about where the money went for very long, simply because it made me mad."

I DECIDED THAT DAY

After this conversation I was determined not to let this happen to myself or anybody I could help. The decisions I made that day are what leads me to share this message with as many people as I possibly can.

Yes, the market can be extremely rewarding during certain periods, but viciously ravaging during others. Investors in the stock market lost almost *half* their interest and their principle in 2001 and *then again* in 2008. Most are just barely getting back to even, having lost all that growth and all that time. Fighting these rollercoaster markets is one of the most stressful things a person getting close to retirement is faced with. Fortunately there are solutions to this, and as we'll see in these chapters, more growth (even a lot more growth) actually happens with consistent, reasonable returns than with wild swings up and down.

Takeaways:

1. Remember experiences you've had in the past where you've suffered losses in the markets (stock, real estate, metals, oil and gas, etc.) and learn as much as you possibly can from those experiences.

2. If you've ever had to deal with a significant monetary loss, think about what was going through your mind at the time. How did you feel? What emotions were running through you? Besides yourself, who else in your family was affected?

3. Hope for the best, but put plans in place to deal with worst case scenarios. It's inevitable that the markets will crash again. Be prepared!

Chapter 2

Lessons For Escaping Loss: A Repeating History

"Those who cannot remember the past are condemned to repeat it..."
- George Santayana

"Study the past, if you would define the future."
- Confucius

REALITY IN THE MARKET

A great majority of people back in 2001 and 2008 had experiences very similar to Nancy and her husband. Anyone who was 65 back in 2001 or 2008 probably took the news the hardest. They were at the peak of their accumulation phase and most of them still had the majority of their money in the markets as they prepared to enter retirement.

It's unfortunate, but anyone who's studied the markets, or paid attention to financial news even just a bit, knows that the markets have a crash or correction about every 7 or so years. We've seen this for the last 100 years, but most recently in 2001 with the dot com bubble, and then we saw it again 7 years later in 2008 with the mortgage bubble and banking crisis. If history repeats itself, as you look ahead another 30 years, there's 4 more major crashes you'll likely see.

THE DOT COM BUBBLE - YEAR 2000

In 1998 and 1999, there was a bubble forming around the hot news of the internet. There was a perceived value of a company taking their business online. Just by putting up a website and adding a dot com to the end of their company name, a company's valuation would shoot up.

This perceived value is one of the things that caused the bubble. Even though there wasn't a whole lot of actual value, it was the perceived, or artificial value that made the ticker symbols rise. However, it wasn't long before reality caught up to investors. In 2000 the markets really started to slide and slide hard. There were 3 years of double digit losses, 2000, 2001, and 2002.

Imagine for a moment all those people who were 65 and getting ready to retire in 2000. Can you imagine what must have been going through their mind by the time 2002 was over? Having lost nearly 45% of their holdings?

THE HOUSING BUBBLE - YEAR 2007

A few years later, we saw another bubble start to form that made the markets perform extremely well. This revolved around the real estate market and the skyrocketing prices and valuations of homes.

In many areas, a home in 2006 cost 40% more than it did in 2004, for the exact same home! There weren't any changes to the home, the yard was the same, the square footage remained consistent and the curb appeal was exactly as it was 2 years earlier. The only difference was the perceived value of the real estate.

Again, just as we saw in 1998, one of the things that caused the bubble was the perceived value. And again, just like we saw in 2000, real values and the writing on the wall caught up with investors in 2008. From the high in 2007 to the low in 2009, the market lost 52%.

...investments in the market had sunk further and faster than ever expected. Oct. 27th, 2008 US News

We can only imagine what was going through people's minds that were near retirement age at this point. Their dreams of retiring were dashed away. And if they were already retired and had kept their money in the market, many of them had to come out of retirement and back into the workforce. Only now, in most cases they weren't able to get back into their same lucrative position they were at before they had retired.

11

The absolute worst age you could have in 1999 was 65. Think of it, in 1999 your money would likely have been the highest it had ever been. But by 2002, you were 68 and had just lost 45% of your wealth. By the time you were 73 in 2007, your money was back up to where it was before the crash of the early 2000's. Maybe you would have retired at that point, but it was probably a good idea if you didn't. Because by the time you were 75 in 2009, your money had been cut in half again. Ouch! If they were in the stock market, the retirement of the people who were supposed hang up their hat in 1999 was completely decimated.

THE QUANTITATIVE EASING BUBBLE - YEAR 2014

Here we are almost 7 years later. As of this writing it's 2014. In many ways we're seeing some of the same behaviors of inexperienced investors that we saw in 1998-99 and in 2006-07. The masses buying on greed in the highest market we've ever seen.

This one has been loosely called the "quantitative easing" bubble. People that are paying attention know that this kind of financial policy can't go on forever. But like we've seen in the past, there is a perceived value taking root in the market.

As we've seen in the past, we have a knowledge for what happens with a bubble due to perceived value... it crashes, or corrects down to its' actual values.

In large part, the perceived value today in the markets is due to the amount of money that's been printed. When $85 billion is being pumped into the financial system each month, one can plainly expect to see growth in the markets. But the question that demands an answer is: *"Is there any real value that's causing the market to rise or is this just printed money?"*

I don't care to speculate on what the markets are doing now, but by reading the news and seeing everything that's going on in the world, it's no wonder many savvy investors and people nearing retirement age are moving good portions of their money away from the market at this point in time.

> ...they're worried that QE is distorting investment decisions and leading to the misallocation of capital, and worried about the losses it would make on behalf of the American investor if there happened to be a sharp fall in the price of the bonds and securities it has bought in the past five years. -The Guardian, Dec. 2013

Anyone who saw their portfolio ravaged by losses in 2001 and 2008 doesn't want to see that again.

Takeaways:

1. Know that the markets are very cyclical. Position yourself so that you're not in the wrong place at the wrong time, like those who were age 65 in 1999.

2. Be cognizant of what history has shown when markets are at all-time highs. When the markets are high, be conscientious of the fact that a correction may be close at hand.

3. Especially as you get closer to the distribution years of your life, or if you're already in retirement, run a quick analysis of what a 45% loss would do to your plans. Can you suffer a loss like that and still maintain the retirement lifestyle you're planning on or currently enjoying?

Chapter 3

The Market Cost Me How Much?

"I suppose if I were to give advice, it would be to keep
out of Wall Street"
- John D. Rockefeller

TRUE COST OF A MARKET LOSS

What many people don't take into consideration while planning
their retirement is that a loss is much different from a gain in terms
of average return or year-to-year calculations and how you *think*
your investments are doing. Losses can have significantly more
impact on your portfolio than gains.

Wall Street still seems to be able to make people believe their
money will actually grow by 12% year after year after year in a
truly compounded fashion. We often hear of incredible rates of
return coming out of Wall Street. You may hear friends,

colleagues, family, or the like, talking about a hot stock or the pile of money they're about to make with the next big thing. But when we look at the numbers, it's simply not the case. On the surface, you think you can just sit in the market and let it ride, earning an average of 12% like what they say, but after running a few simple calculations, you'll truly understand what's going on with your money.

Consider the following hypothetical example of Wall Street's fuzzy math:

Tom has $100,000 in the market and gets a whopping 100% return in one year, skyrocketing his holdings to $200,000. But in year two, the tide turns and the market loses 50%, he's now back down to $100,000. In year three, he makes a 100% return again and is back on top with $200,000. But by the end of year four, he's lost 50% again, taking him back to down to $100,000.

Year	Market	Starting Bal.	Ending Bal.
1	+100%	$100,000	$200,000
2	-50%	$200,000	$100,000
3	+100%	$100,000	$200,000
4	-50%	$200,000	$100,000

The fuzzy math is that, over the four year period of time, Tom averaged a 25% rate of return. And this is average rate of return that is purported by Wall Street. They're constantly touting 12% returns or 15% returns. But how much money does Tom actually have? The exact same amount he had when he started! He may have averaged 25% rate of return, but he realized zero growth on his money! It's easy to understand why so many people get confused about what is actually happening to their retirement money.

Imagine for a moment that you were 64 in early 2000 and you had a $1,000,000 retirement nest egg in the markets. By the time you were 67, after 3 years of double digit losses, you now had $598,804. At this point, what's going through your mind? A rosy retirement picture probably isn't the first thing that pops into your mind. In most cases, people went back to work, and if you left your money in the market and kept contributing about $15,000 per year for another 4 years, you had built it up to $1,049,664.

By the time you were 72, it was the year 2007. If you didn't make any change and just kept it in the market, by the end of 2008, your retirement nest egg would be down again to around $645,648 and you'd be 73 years old. What are your options at this point? Most people scaled back their retirement dreams, and started their "golden years" quite a bit less "golden" than they had worked so hard for. It was the reality they were faced with. Time off, travel, hobbies, spending significant time with family and friends would have to be scaled back for these people. See the following chart to get an understanding of what the numbers looked like.

Year	Age	Retirement Nest Egg
1999	64	$1,000,000
2000	65	$898,600
2001	66	$781,422
2002	67	$598,804
2003	68	$771,768
2004	69	$841,150
2005	70	$866,384
2006	71	$999,386
2007	72	$1,049,664
2008	73	$645,648

But it doesn't stop there. Let's take a look at what these market losses have cost investors over the last 15 years and what they will continue to cost over the next 20 to 40 years. Not only do we have to factor in the monetary losses in 2001 and 2008, but we also have to factor in the time loss and the opportunity losses. If the money took 5 years to come back, that's 5 years we could have been compounding. If we saw this twice in the last 15 years, that's 10 years we could have been growing our wealth. This is why the 2000's were termed the lost decade.

But Wall Street has a unique way of making people feel good after a loss. You've heard it said, "It will come back, just hold out and be patient." Which is fine, but what about for people who are in retirement, or close to retirement that just aren't in a position to "hold out" and "be patient" waiting for their money to return to previous highs? What if they were counting on that money they just lost to supplement their income?

Market losses are often looked at as just a loss on paper, but that couldn't be further from the truth. If someone has $500k and loses 52% like we saw from the high in 2007 to the low in 2009, that $250k loss is gone, and never to be used by that investor again. They'll have to start compounding again with the remaining money.

Let me show you how much a stock market loss can really cost. But let me start with some of the Wall Street propaganda. They say when you're young, you can afford to take losses because you have time to make up for those losses. They claim that, when you're young, losses don't hurt you as much as when you're older because you've got plenty of time. Would it surprise you to learn that this isn't entirely true?

Probably not. However, what might surprise you is seeing that the exact opposite is true. There is an incredible cost with principal loss. Losses at any time are not good, but they can be even more costly when you are young. Let me illustrate with an example.

Let's say that, during a downturn in the stock market, you lost $50,000 when you were 45 years old. Also assume that you could have averaged a rate of return of 7% over the next 20 years, until the age of sixty five. If the loss hadn't occurred, you could have compounded that $50,000 until age 65. What's shocking is that this $50,000 loss really cost you $193,484 by age 65. How much better off could you be? How much more comfortable in your retirement can you be with this additional $193,484 sitting in your coffers? To say it's frustrating and aggravating is an understatement. This is why you *cannot* lose money, even it is just 'on paper' as they say.

Let's take it one step further. Is it likely you live to only 65? Probably not. If we run the numbers out until age 85 which is a typical life expectancy, it's almost enough to make your stomach turn. Let's say you lived until you were 85 and could have continued to compound that $50,000 for 40 years instead of 20. At 7% that same $50,000 loss would have turned into $748,222. Yes, you're reading that right…$748,222 is what you would have had at age 85 if you hadn't suffered a $50,000 loss at age 45. How much better off would your family be with that extra $750,000? How much easier would retirement be with an extra 3/4 of a million sitting at your disposal? How much more can you leave as your legacy if you don't suffer any losses? What if this $750,000 is left in a trust specifically designed to pay for college education?

So that $50,000 loss wasn't JUST a $50,000 loss. In fact it cost you nearly 3/4 of a million dollars. Pretty hefty price to pay for dabbling in the markets. Again, this is why it's critical you never lose your principal...ever. For this reason alone, you should get the money you can't afford to lose out of the market or other vehicles that are subject to loss.

Takeaways:

1. Know the difference between average rate of return and compounded rate of return. Assumptions using an average rate of return never take into consideration the impact a loss will have on the actual dollar amount you'll realize in your account over time.

2. Understand that the true cost of a market loss doesn't just include the present dollar amount. You also need to consider the time that's lost. How many years did it require you to work to save the amount of money you lost? What would your accounts look like today if you had never experienced a loss?

3. Realize the money lost in a market crash or correction is gone forever. You may hear people say it took 7 years for me to get my money back after a crash, but that isn't the money they lost. That is new money they had to compound and earn. The money that was lost cannot be compounded for the future. Know that there is an opportunity loss that comes with every market loss.

Chapter 4

The Compound Corrosion
Of Fees

"The miracle of compounding returns is overwhelmed by the
tyranny of compounding costs."

- John Bogle

We really can't have a discussion about market losses, without
addressing the fees that are often associated with accounts that are
in the stock market. A colleague of mine tells a story that
illustrates several key points. As a financial professional, he was
working with a physician on some of his retirement planning and
they were reviewing an IRA where this client had built up a
considerable portion of his assets. He had a balance totaling just
over 1 million dollars. After looking at how this particular IRA
had performed over the last 15 years, things were just not adding
up.

The doctor hadn't contributed to this account in about 10 years, but it was still hovering around the same dollar amount for the same period of time. In effect, it hadn't grown a bit over the last 10 years. Although his statements showed moderate returns, the dollar amounts weren't reflecting those returns.

My colleague asked him how much he was paying in fees, to which the doctor replied around $250.00 per year. He asked him if he was sure that was his only fee, which the doctor assured him it was. After going through the statement with a fine toothed comb and on the last page, my colleague showed this doctor something he didn't want to see, a total of *3% in portfolio management fees*. He said the doctor about choked.

After 10 years of trying to grow this money, he had paid 3% per year in management fees. On 1 million dollars, that is not $250.00 per year. He came to the realization very quickly as to why he wasn't any further ahead than he was 10 years previous. He had paid $300,000 in FEES!

A 401k, IRA or any other account that is being handled by a manager typically has a management fee of between 0.5%-3%, sometimes even higher. Depending on the services and trades that are being made, these fees can vary substantially. What's important is to find out exactly how much in fees you're paying. Normally it takes some research and some digging, but you've got to remove the devastation that management fees have on your money. See the following example of a fee schedule. In this example the fees are extremely high, however, it's not that uncommon to see fees like this. In this example you'll see a total of 3.54% in fees!

A small percentage fee each year may not sound like much, but that's one of Wall Street biggest lies. For example sake, assume you're invested in a fund that has a gross annual return of 7% and to be conservative, let's say you're only being charged a 2% annual fee. What this means is that over your investing lifetime, instead of earning 7%, you earned 5%. The end results are staggering. In all reality, you've lost close to 2/3 of what you would have had. How can this be? The difference in actual return was only 2%, which is under 1/3 of the total rate of the return. How did you lose 2/3 when the fee was under 1/3 of the total return? Wouldn't the most you could have lost be under 1/3? The answer, shockingly, is no. The reason is because of compound interest.

Let's look at an example. Take $100,000 compounded at 7% for an investing lifetime of 50 years. The answer comes to $2,945,703. Now let's look at what the same $100,000 looks like after the fees. $100,000 compounded for 50 years at just 5%. I know it's an unpleasant truth, but the answer is $1,146,740. Because of the compounding interest, over 60% of your money went to the IRA or 401k fund manager.

Starting Bal. at age 40	Average Interest Rate	Interest Rate after Fees	Total Percent of Fees
$100,000	7%	5%	2%

After lifetime from age 40-90	Total Amount earned at 7%	Amount to Investor after Fees	Fees to 401k / IRA company
	$2,945,703	$1,146,740	-$1,798,963

As you compound your interest, you're also compounding your costs. What's sad is that most Americans aren't aware of this, or haven't had the opportunity to learn this. It can be seen pretty clearly with a compound interest table. But consider the terms of this transaction, you as the investor are putting up 100% of the capital, you're taking 100% of the risk, and you're only getting 40% of the returns in the end. It's mind numbing! Again, think this through. You're putting up 100% of the capital, you're taking 100% of the risk and you're only receiving 40% of the money. How they get away with so much, makes you wonder who they're paying off! Knowledge is power, but only if it's acted upon. Now that you're informed, do everything in your power to reduce fees on your retirement accounts. Don't you deserve the $2,945,703 instead of the $1,146,740?

If we look at how much the annual fee is in relation to our gain or loss for the year, it gets even more ridiculous. With an account of $100,000 that earned 7% in one year, you've got earnings of $7,000. Let's say there is a management fee of 2%. We take the cost of the fees ($2,140) and divide that by the amount of money we earned ($7,000) and we get 31%. Our fees were actually 31% of our earnings for that year, not 2% which is what the typical investor thinks it is.

Account Bal.	7% Return	-2% Fees	5% Net Return
$100,000	$7,000	-$2,140	$4,860

-$2,140 Fee / $7000 Return = -30.5% of Total Earnings

In this example, the fees equal 31% of the growth. This is a steep price to pay, especially over the course of many years. It's no wonder we have a retirement crisis on our hands in America. All the money that would have typically gone to the investor, is going to 401k or IRA company.

What about in years where the markets are down and you show a loss for the year? Do you still pay the management fee? The answer is yes! You're still paying that management even in years like 2008 when the markets tanked. If there was a -38% loss that year, it was actually -40% after the management company took their cut.

Whether you win or lose each year, the management company always gets their cut. They always win when it comes to fees they collect. What you need to be aware of, is how these fees impact your growth over the long run.

Don't get me wrong, in no way am I saying these companies should work for free. I'm all for American businesses to make healthy and sizeable profits, but by building up, elevating and bringing massive amounts of value and knowledge to their customers. Not by flat out stealing from them because they're unaware of the devastation that the compounded fees are having on their accounts.

Hedge fund managers earn billions of dollars each year. In some sense, it's because they're on the winning end of the fees and compound interest game. The 25 highest-earning hedge fund managers in the United States took home a total of $21.15 billion in compensation in 2013.

Isn't it time you put a stop to this and started to put this money back in your own pocket? I'm sure you're not okay with being legally robbed. Take action on this and put a stop to it today by finding out how much you're paying in fees. Also know that you may get a smoke screen when you first contact your fund manager in relation to fees. Unfortunately, at first, they may give you an answer that sounds reasonable, but after you continue to dig do you find all the annual percentage fees.

It's critical you examine all the fees that are being levied on your retirement accounts. It's vital for your well-being and the well-being of your loved ones. Most people rarely look at their accounts and just assume they're doing fine. They fail to inspect what they expect with their 401k, IRA or other managed account. Don't be one of these people who have their head in the sand.

Takeaways:

1. Pull out your monthly, quarterly, or annual statement and add up all the fees that are being charged to your 401k, IRA or other account that is in the stock market

2. Know that because of compound interest, these fees can eat up to 60% or more of what you could have accumulated over a lifetime.

Chapter 5

Inflation: A Thief In The Night

"Bankers know that history is inflationary and that money is the
last thing a wise man will hoard."

- William Durant

If we look at the rule of 72, we see the power of compound interest.
We know exactly how long it will take for our money to double,
double and again, and then double again. It's a simple math
equation that Albert Einstein is credited for discovering.

We take the number 72 and divide by an interest rate. The answer
is the number of years it will take for our money to double. For
example, 72 divided by a 6% interest rate, gives us 12 years. If we
have $100,000 growing at 6%, we know that it will turn into
$200,000 in 12 years. Easy!

> Take the number 72 and divide by the interest rate you're earning. The answer is how many years it will take for your money to double.

The rule of 72 also works against us with inflation. If the inflation rate is 4%, assuming what the government says is correct, then we know our money is going to lose value to the tune of 4% per year. It's been said that inflation is actually much higher than 4%, but for simplicity sake, let's call it an average of 4%. If we go to the rule of 72, we can see how much our money will be worth in the future. We take 72 and divide that by the inflation rate of 4%. We get 18 years. Effectively, what this means is that our money will buy 50% less in 18 years than what it will buy today. $100 worth of groceries today will only buy $50 worth of groceries in 18 years. These are pretty conservative numbers, the inflation rate may actually be more than 4%.

What it means is this: In order to keep up with inflation, and be able to buy the same amount of goods and services in the future with the money we have, we'll have to get at least 4% interest on our nest egg. If we have $100,000 now, we'll need to get 4% on our money over the next 18 years to get the same amount of goods and services that $100,000 will buy today.

Take a look at these examples of inflation:

Movie Ticket

1954	1984	2014
$.50	$3.50	$8.00

A Loaf of Bread

1954	1984	2014
$.16	$.51	$2.97

Gallon of Gas

1954	1984	2014
$.20	$1.24	$3.53

Candy Bar

1954	1984	2014
$.05	$.40	$1.10

So how does this affect our retirement funds? Basically, if we have our money in money market accounts, cd's, savings accounts, under the mattress, or in any other vehicle that's not earning at least 4% (again, assuming inflation is only 4%), we're effectively losing 4% of its' buying power every single year.

If someone has $100,000 and is 47 now, and they aren't doing anything with their money but letting it sit idly, not earning anything, it will only have $50,000 worth of buying power at retirement age. In another 18 years, at age 83, the same $100,000 will only buy the equivalent of $25,000 worth of goods and services.

72 and divided by the inflation rate helps you know how much income you'll need to plan for.

Inflation Rate	Years	Age	Annual Income today
72/4	18	47	$100,000
			Will Be Like
		65	$50,000
		83	$25,000

So how do we plan for this? You've got to get an interest rate that not only helps you keep up with inflation, but also helps you reduce the amount of money by which you'll be depleting your nest egg. To keep numbers easy, if you've got $500,000 earning 10% per year, you can take $60,000 in year one of your retirement and only reduce your nest egg by $10,000.

During your working career, your wages or salary usually increase to meet the rising costs of goods and services, and generally, your earnings are keeping pace with inflation. But when you're not earning a salary, it becomes all the more important to plan for how you're going to come up with these lost increases. Otherwise inflation will literally rob you of your lifestyle.

Most retirees fail to measure the consequences of inflation, which can be a damaging impact to their dignity and freedom. Examples of this abound. Consider the couple who is 85 years old today. When they retired 20 years ago, they believed they would be just fine with a total retirement income of $24,000 per year for the rest of their lives. In 1994, this was a decent to live on for all their basic needs. Their home was paid off, and their cars were paid off and still in pretty good working order. All they needed to plan for was utilities, real estate taxes, food, entertainment, gas for the car, and a few other variable expenses. In many months, they'd even have money left over which they could set aside and use for travel or other frivolous spending.

When they retired, the price of a first class stamp was $.29, a gallon of gas cost $1.11 (as gas fluctuates considerably), and a dozen eggs was $.87. Compare that with what prices are as of this writing in 2014. A first class stamp is $.49, a 41% increase from 1994. The average price of a gallon of gas is $3.53, a 69% increase from 1994. Today, a dozen eggs runs about $1.90, which is a 55% increase. Their buying power was effectively cut in half.

Where they once had $200-$300 left over at the end of the month, they're now coming up short $700-$800 each month. What once was a decent and care free retirement for them, is now a stressful and scary existence. They're now faced with problems they didn't think they'd have to deal with.

A quick jaunt down memory lane will help illustrate this further. Remember back to when you purchased your first home, how much did it cost? If you were like many, for the first few years, you were concerned with how you were going to make the monthly payments. An average purchase price for a home in 1974 was around $36,000. Or think back to when you purchased your first car, do you remember how much you paid for it? The average cost of a car in 1965 was $2,700.

Today, the average price of a home is $230,000 and the average car is $29,000. How things have changed! These prices seem outrageous compared to what prices once were.

If we take a step into the future and run a few simple math equations, we can get an idea for what things will cost in the future. At 4% inflation, the price of a week's worth of groceries ($50) in 2044 will be approximately $160. Almost 3 times as much! The average monthly utility bills ($250) will be $810 per month. A movie ticket will most likely set you back about $40. A dinner out in the restaurant will be around $130 and the average gallon of gas will be around $12.

Again this is at a modest inflation rate of 4%. We can only hope we don't see inflation like we did in the late 70's and early 80's. If inflation looks anything like it did during that time period 4% is going to look like a walk in the park.

Is it any wonder we see more and more retirees going back out into the workforce? Take a stroll through fast food restaurants, retail stores, Wal-Mart, etc. and you'll notice droves and droves of people who've had to go back to work. One of the reasons they're back to work is because they've taken a beating on the buying power of their money. They've got to earn in today's dollars because what they set aside in yesterday's dollars is only buying about half of what they need.

Takeaways:

1. Understand that inflation is very real and will put a halt to your retirement dreams if it's not considered and planned for.

2. Don't underestimate the amount of interest you'll need to earn on your money in order to keep up with and beat inflation.

Part Two

FORTUNATELY, THERE IS SOME GOOD NEWS

Chapter 6

Securing the Foundation

The wise man built his house upon a rock...

- Matthew 7:24

So what's the solution to all of these perils we face today? How do we avoid losses, save ourselves from the damaging impact of annual percentage fees, yet still get the returns we need in order to outpace and beat inflation? Gratefully there is a solution.

It might shock you to know that the cornerstone of the Millionaire Safety Secret has actually been around for hundreds of years. However, only for the last 30 years has it been packaged in such a way that investors are using it in the way I'm going to describe.

How can something be a secret if it's been around for hundreds of years? For many of the 30 years it's been available, it's only been accessible to large institutional investors such as banks that could invest at least $100,000,000. Merrill Lynch, Citigroup, Credit Suisse Bank, First Boston, Wells Fargo, and Berkshire Hathaway have all financed or invested in this concept. But there hasn't been an ideal platform where it's been offered to non-institutional investors until the last 10 years.

Fortunately things have progressed to a point where others can participate quite easily. It's good to know there are strategies available that get very good rates of return, even high double-digit returns, but that do not have market risks. You have other options than just the market that is loaded with risk and fees!

This concept is one that these institutions and other larger investors have been using for the last 30 years to protect themselves from the peril of losses and lost opportunity in the market. Berkshire Hathaway has been pouring hundreds of millions into this concept and has averaged very good returns over the last 10 years. While markets were tumbling and the masses were losing 30%-50% during 2008 that they would never be able to use again, others were quietly getting good returns in this strategy, stockpiling away their principal and their returns each year.

It's known as an Insurance Settlement Investment and it's actually very simple. Not only is it simple, but it's very reasonable to achieve consistent returns of between 7%-9% year after year without worry about losses in the stock market. Over the last 14 years, the actual returns have been higher than 7%-9% and closer to 14% per year. It's even possible to do 40%-50% in a year with this concept! But conservative consistency is what we're after. It's amazing what you can do with 7%-9% gains year over year when you don't have to worry about losing those gains or the principal.

An Insurance Settlement is where a person, normally in their 80's who no longer wants or needs a portion or their entire life insurance

45

policy can sell it on the open market. On the open market, they can get more from investors than what the insurance company is willing to pay them if they cashed it in. As investors, a trust is formed, and we purchase their unwanted policy. We become the owners and beneficiaries of the proceeds upon the death of the insured. The seller of the policy gets more cash today than what the insurance company is willing to pay them if they cashed it out, and the buyer, or investor, gets to receive a sizeable return when the insured passes away.

If the insured person had a $10mm death benefit policy and could get $1.2 from the insurance company by cashing it in, they might be able to get $2mm on the open market from a collective group of investors. If they're set on getting cash for it today, it only makes sense for them to get as much for it as possible. As investors, we collectively put in a total of $2mm and upon the maturity of the insured, we collectively get $10mm.

There are several reasons why Insurance Settlement Investments are one of the best tools a person can have in their retirement portfolio. One reason is the consistent return on investment. There is considerable equity built into the contract that allows for sizeable, consistent returns. Another reason is because of the safety. You'll never have to worry about losing time, energy, opportunity, and money when the stock market goes down. We'll go into this in some more detail, but simplicity, security, value, and liquidity are several other reasons these are an incredible financial tool.

An Insurance Settlement is a non-correlated asset class, meaning it's not correlated in any way to the stock market, real estate, precious metals, oil and gas or any other market that has volatile up and down swings. They are contractual agreements and in many cases have built-in contractual returns. They're also backed by some of the largest, most secure insurance organizations in the world, companies that have been around for over one hundred years that are in the business of protecting people against loss. On top of all this, and to add to the security, they're usually held within a trust.

Also, one of the most important factors of insurance settlement investments is that there aren't any ongoing annual percentage fees! The trust company doesn't charge the typical .5% - 3% management fee that a stock market fund manager charges. The trust company does have a fee, but only on accounts that are considered an IRA, and it's small, typically under $200 per year. Cash accounts typically have ZERO annual fee!

Plus, when there's a downturn and investors in the markets are losing money in leaps and bounds, insurance settlements are safely tucked away in a trust. Instead of losing money due to market volatility, investors in insurance settlements have nothing to worry about, because their money isn't in the market at all. It's secured away into a trust where the money will be when they need to start accessing it.

When it comes to creating certainty and rock solid stability in these uncertain times, there's no better way than to move money out of markets that fluctuate wildly and into strategies that have contractual obligations against loss.

Takeaways:

1. Insurance Settlement Investments have been used for the last 30 years, but only until about 10 years ago have they been available to non-institutional investors.

2. Insurance Settlement Investments provide market-like returns (7%-14% annually) but without the market risks. They're a stable, consistent investment that are bound by contracts.

Chapter 7

Back To Simplicity For Consistent Returns

There is no greatness where there is no simplicity,
goodness and truth.
- Leo Tolstoy

"Any intelligent fool can make things bigger, more complex, and
more violent. It takes a touch of genius — and a lot of courage —
to move in the opposite direction.
- E.F. Schumacher

Insurance Settlements can be a very lucrative investment. For the
last 14 years they've averaged double digit returns. But one of the
most incredible things about insurance settlements is the simplicity
they offer. An investor can know what's involved and how the
returns are achieved very quickly and easily.

Webster defines simplicity as the quality of being easy to
understand or use. It's only common sense to invest in things that
are easy to understand and use, things that satisfy a need of the
market place and where the numbers are laid out in black and

white, things that don't include too many variables or moving parts. In addition to the returns they've averaged, the simplicity of the investment is one of the reasons they have become one of the go-to strategies for people managing the responsibility of their own retirement.

Simple Investing vs Complexity

For so many, the options available for investing are limited to vehicles that carry significant risks and that aren't the easiest to understand. As we've discussed, the majority of workers in America have invested into their company 401k's or other IRA's. These funds are then commonly allocated to a myriad of complex mutual funds, of which, the employee usually has no understanding.

Their money is directly invested in the stock market that is laden with large amounts of extensive risk. We've seen this risk as we've looked at the major losses that were suffered in 2001 and in 2008.

While it may make sense to take advantage of an employer match, it definitely doesn't make sense to take unnecessary risks with these retirement funds, especially when there isn't a way to easily understand the individual companies they're investing in, nor the time to do the extensive research this would require.

The problem is that sometimes employees don't know of any other options or where else to put their money. They've been told time and time again that in order to get a return, there has to significant risks. They also see their cohorts doing the same thing, so why not join in?

An Easier Way

In reality, however, all that is needed to get a good return is a sensible and easy to understand investment where the terms are laid out in black and white, and where they can see how everyone involved is to benefit or get value. Options that are clear and easy to understand, and where the universal law of bringing value to others is hard at work. We can find these things in Insurance Settlements.

It's a time tested law of business that when we bring value and service to others, we inherently bring value to ourselves. This law is what makes commerce and prosperity go around. Allow me to go into this further and explain how this is applicable in insurance settlement investing and how easy it is to see what's involved.

Judith and Adam

Let me illustrate with a story. Judith and Adam worked hard their entire lives and had built up a sizeable estate. They started with nothing at the age of twenty five when they were married. Paycheck to paycheck is how it seemed to go when they were young and as their children started to come along.

But Adam was industrious. He worked hard at his craft and started to become an extremely valuable member to the market place. He worked his way up through the corporate ladder and by the time he and Judith were 60, Adam had become the CEO of a midsize company. Part of the compensation package he was given as the CEO included a permanent life insurance policy with a 10 million dollar death benefit.

The company would pay the premiums on this life insurance policy and allow the cash value to build up, then when Adam retired he would be able to keep the policy as his own, including all the cash value. The only stipulation was that when he retired, he would have to be the one to make the premium payments.

Time came and went and he served his company, the clients of his company and his employees to the best of his ability. He loved what he did and worked well beyond the typical retirement age. He was now 75, ready to completely retire and hang up the many hats he wore as CEO. But he wasn't quite sure what to do with this life insurance policy that had been part of his compensation package.

Their estate didn't have an immediate need for the 10 million dollar death benefit. He had set aside plenty to cover the estate taxes upon his death. Adam's children were smart and self-reliant people. They had been very involved with the estate planning and were already going to be receiving a very sizeable inheritance. Adam didn't have any outstanding debts or liabilities that would need to be paid upon his passing.

He thought about it for a while, and he was on the verge of calling the insurance company and cashing it out, but then he thought about the nice gesture it would be to surprise Judith with this as a special gift. So he decided to continue to pay the premiums, keep it in force and revisit what to do with it later.

After 5 years, he was glad he had kept it in force. Judith started to go downhill and was later diagnosed with Alzheimer's disease. He knew that if anything happened to him or if he suddenly passed away, the life insurance policy would help in covering Judith's long term care costs.

Time went on and Judith's life ended quite peacefully. After some time, Adam, who was now 85, decided it would be a good idea to meet with his adviser and get his financial house in order. His adviser asked again what he would like to do with this life insurance policy.

Somewhat hesitant about keeping it and continuing the pay the annual premiums, he re-evaluated how much his company had invested into it and how much he had invested in it over the years. They looked at how much cash was available in it. Between what his company had put into it and what he himself had put into it totaled about $750,000. The total amount of cash value he could take out was about $1,250,000.

He decided to move forward and take the cash. He figured the only reason he was keeping it in force was as a gift to Judith. With her now passed on, he saw no other reason to keep making the premium payments.

Other Options Are Available

Instead of cashing it in to the insurance company, his adviser mentioned he might be able to get a better price for it on the open market. Somewhat shocked, Adam asked how that would be possible. He had no idea there was an open market for unwanted life insurance policies.

Like most people, he had never looked outside his company 401k and compensation package. His adviser explained that with the amount of equity built into life insurance policies (in his case, likely $7,500,000+) investors are willing to pay more cash to the insured than the insurance company will offer, because now they can become the legal beneficiaries of the death benefit.

Adam was a smart business man. If he could get more cash for the same policy from somewhere else, he wanted to do just that. His adviser listed it on the open market, and came into contact with a trust company that wanted to pursue the purchase. After some underwriting, and paperwork, it was decided that the trust company would pay $4,000,000 for his policy.

Win / Win or Benefit / Benefit

With an offer of $2,750,000 more than the insurance company was going to pay, Adam was ecstatic to finalize the transaction. After the money was received into escrow, Adam signed the ownership and the rights to the death benefit over to the trust company. He received his $4,000,000 and spent the rest of his life enjoying and giving away just about as much money as he wanted. And the trust company were now the legal and rightful owners of the death benefit of $10,000,000.

This story of Adam and Judith is just one example. But there are thousands and thousands of wealthy seniors that no longer want or need their life insurance, and who would rather have cash for it today. If they can easily get more for it on the open market than what the insurance company is willing to pay, it only makes practical sense for them to do so.

Unique Simplicity

The simplicity of this investment is unique. It satisfies the need of a growing market place full of boomers who are getting closer and closer to the age where they may want to sell their life insurance policies for cash today. Value is given in exchange for value and the buyer and seller benefit together. Seniors who sell their policy get to receive a larger portion of money today than the insurance company is willing to pay, that they can then use to continue a lifestyle they're comfortable with. They can use that money for a second or third home, for traveling, doing their hobbies, or anything they'd like. And the buyer gets to enjoy a very good return on their investment.

In our story, the value that was brought to Adam was the additional money he could get above and beyond what the insurance company was willing to pay. He could now use this money however he chose. The value the investors received was the right to be the owners of the policy and the beneficiaries of the death benefit, safely growing and compounding their money by an average of 11-14% each year in a vehicle that's not correlated in any way to the Wall Street casino.

Warren Buffett is famous for advising people not to invest in anything they don't understand with exact clarity. Yet this is what most Americans do every day. In so many cases, they'll invest in mutual funds that are spread across hundreds and hundreds of companies. It's almost impossible to know and understand the nature and profitability of each company. Or they'll invest in gold and silver without understanding the supply and demand at the time. This is one of the pitfalls people make with their retirement accounts. They simply don't understand exactly where their money is or what they're actually invested in.

One of the beauties of Insurance Settlements is that they're easy to understand from start to finish. It's one of the many reasons Warren Buffett has been using this exact strategy for the last 10 years. It's something he and his shareholders can understand very easily. It's a transaction that benefits from a universal business law of exchanging value for value and filling a need in the market place. They know exactly what the payout is going to be and have a reasonable time frame for when it will pay out.

Takeaways:

1. You can remove stress and anxiety about your money by understanding with exact clarity the investments you're involved with. Insurance Settlement Investments are very simple, they're laid out in black and white and you know exactly where your money is and what it's doing.

2. By clearly and easily understanding your investments, you empower yourself to make good decisions. Having a lack of knowledge and information or 'burying your head in the sand' when it comes to your investment strategy, is a surefire way to lose money.

Chapter 8

Getting Down To The Dollars And Cents

The whole is more than the sum of its parts.

- Aristotle

Numbers constitute the only universal language.

- Nathanael West

With more and more people coming to know that there is a way to get more money for their unwanted insurance policy, there are more and more policies coming available to investors. Typically an investor in insurance settlements will have money in only a handful of policies as they start out. But there are insurance settlement funds that are arranged by the trust company that allow investors to participate in multiple policies.

Over the space of a few years, a single investor might have money in 20 different policies. In five years they might have ownership in 50 different policies. When one of those policy matures, the payout is made and the investor can do as they please with their payout.

If they're in the distribution phase of retirement, typically they'll take a portion of the payout to spend and live on or do as they want, and they'll also take a portion to buy into additional policies and reinvest. If they don't need the money to live on, they'll usually put the principle, plus the entire gain back into policies and continue to grow and compound their money.

As you can see, over the course of 5 years or so, if you've got money in 50 different policies at one time, you'll typically have multiple payouts per year. This is how investors create an income stream from insurance settlements. After 10 years, it's common to have ownership in 100 or more different policies and have even more payouts throughout the year.

Nuts and Bolts

Let's take a few examples of typical policies that are available for investment and go through the nuts and bolts. A wealthy 81 year old insured has multiple policies on herself, her husband passed away and she is wanting cash for one of her policies. Through one of her advisers she comes in contact with the trust group, she goes through the underwriting process and it comes back that she's got a 6 year life expectancy.

One of her policies has a death benefit amount of $5.2mm and after the underwriting it's decided by the trust that she can be offered $2mm today for her policy. She's happy as can be, as this is much more than the insurance company could pay. The insurance company is happy as well because they'll continue to receive the premium payments.

So she gladly accepts, receives the $2mm and signs ownership rights and beneficiary rights over to the trust. The trust sets aside 6 years' worth of premium payments into escrow, plus an additional 12 months for buffer. The policy is then made available for investment. If an investor puts in $20,000 and buys into this particular policy, the contractual obligation to this investor upon maturity will be approximately $33,750.

Notice a few things. There is money set aside by the trust company to pay premiums on this policy for over 7 years. If the insured passes away before that period of time, there will be money left in the escrow account which is dispersed to the investor.

What this means is that if the insured passes away in 2 years, there will be over 5 years' worth of escrowed premiums that will come back to the investor. In this particular example, with a $20,000 investment, let's say there was $2,750 escrowed for premium payments.

Because the insured passed away in 2 years, it means there was only 2 years' worth of escrowed premium used to pay the insurance company, which in this example, would equate to approximately $750. The other $2,000 would be returned to the investor in addition to their contractual maturity payment of $33,750.

In this example, the investor saw an early maturity. Their $20,000 turned into $35,750 in a matter of 2 years, which is a 79% total return. It took 2 years to get there, so the annual return would be 39%. It doesn't always happen like this, and as investors, we don't expect this to happen, but it can happen and does happen with some frequency.

More normally, however, the insured will pass away at or around the life expectancy. In our example, it was 6 years. To run through this scenario, the investor will receive the contractual obligation at payout which is $33,750 plus the one year worth of unused escrowed premium of $375, a total of $34,125.

So the original $20,000 turned into $34,125 in 6 years. The total return is 70%. But to get an annual return we divide the 70% by 6 years to get an annual return of close to 12%. This is the scenario that you'll see happen most regularly as an investor. These are the kinds of returns that are most typical.

It's wise to go into any investment with low expectations. It's always best to hope for the best, but plan for and anticipate the worst. This way you're always ready and generally content with whatever happens.

With insurance settlement investments, it's wise to go into it with expectations of around 7%-9% per year, you're still in an investment where your money is in a trust and WILL NOT lose value when the stock market tanks, you're in an investment that doesn't have an ongoing annual percentage fee of between .05%-3%. Plus, with a 7%-9% annual return you're still abundantly winning the inflation battle. Then, when it matures on time with 11%-12% returns, you can be extremely happy, and when you get an early maturity, with gains of 35%-40% you can be ecstatic!

However, I'll be the first to admit that there aren't some risks with insurance settlement investments, even though they are very limited. But let's put everything out on the table. You've been around the block enough times to know that there aren't any magic pills or silver bullets. There's not one perfect investment that is completely risk free and bullet proof. You can get close to a perfect investment for what you're trying to accomplish, but inherently there will be some kind of risk with every single tool in the financial toolbox.

It's no different with insurance settlement investments. The number one, biggest risk is if the insured lives significantly longer than the life expectancy. But as we all know, there are two things that are certain in life, death and taxes. We all know we will be taxed and that no one gets out of this life alive. Death is inescapable, nevertheless, we don't have a crystal ball as to when we'll die. Through modern technology, however, and understanding the law of large numbers, by using life expectancy tables and extensive underwriting, and then having multiple doctors examine in great detail the current health and the health history of someone, some very accurate predictions can be made. It's with these tools that a life expectancy is determined. Like I mentioned, the risk is very limited and you can take several steps to reduce the exposure even more, but just know this is part of the deal. I'll go into just how long the insured will typically have to live in order for the investor to lose money and you'll see what I mean when I say the risk is very limited.

Let's go back to our example and play out a scenario of the insured living significantly longer than their life expectancy. In our example the investor bought into a policy with $20,000 on an 81 year old insured. With all the medications she's on, her current medical conditions and her previous health history, the doctors determined her life expectancy to be 6 years.

As a precautionary measure, the trust set aside 7 years' worth of premium in escrow. If she lives until 88, the investors and part owners in this policy will need to come out of pocket for another years' worth of premium. In this example, the amount that would be due is $375 for the year. If she lives until 89, another $375 would be due, and so on until the insured passes away.

This is the only variable in the whole equation. Let's compare it to owning a rental property. If you had a house with renters in it, and the pipes in the kitchen broke, as the landlord, you'd have to come out of pocket to fix the pipes. You might expect to have some of these repairs every year as the owner of the house for as long as you live.

What's different about insurance settlements, is that you know you won't have to come out of pocket with any expenses for a predetermined certain number of years, it will be limited if you do have to come out of pocket, and it will only last in most cases just a few short years. Another difference is that because you know beforehand what will be required and when it will be required, you can plan accordingly. With our example of a rental property, you really have no idea what will happen, how much it will cost, or when it will happen. It's difficult to plan if you don't know what to expect.

Insurance settlement investments are considered a safe strategy because you're money doesn't have significant risk for capital loss like it does in the stock market. Let's see from our example what it would take for you to break even or lose capital.

Again the insured is 81 years old with a life expectancy of 6 years. There are 7 years' worth of premiums set aside in escrow. If the insured lived until 88, a payment of $375 for the year would be due. To figure the breakeven point, or the year in which you would be in the negative, you take the contractual payout at maturity, which in this case, is $33,750, then you subtract the original investment of $20,000 and you get an answer of $13,750, which is the contractual growth on the investment. Now you take the $13,750 and divide that by the annual payment of $375. You get an answer of 36.6. What this means is that the insured would have to live 36.6 years past the age of 88 for you to break even.

Obviously living until age 124 is pretty unlikely! As you can see, there is some risk, but it's very limited.

The trick is to know what the risk is so you can plan ahead. Most settlement trust companies will provide this information on each one of their policies. It's very common to know the life expectancy of the insured and how much will be set aside in escrow for future premium payments. It's also very common to have a good idea of how much your portion of the premium payments will be on an annual basis. Once you've got these numbers, it's extremely easy to mitigate the risk.

Obviously you know that not all the policies you'll have ownership in will mature early and give you incredible, high double-digit returns, but you also know that not all of your policies will mature late, requiring you to set aside a few dollars in reserve to take care of any future premiums that might come due.

You can reasonably expect the majority of your policies to mature on time. You might have 70% of your policies mature on time, with 15% maturing early and 15% maturing late. Those that mature early and put off exceptional returns, will offset those that mature late and in the end balance out the portfolio.

Takeaways:

1. Go into Insurance Settlement Investments with a reasonable expectation of 7%-9% annual returns. With these kinds of returns you're still abundantly winning the inflation battle, you're not giving up more than half your earnings to management fees and you're in a vehicle that is PROTECTED FROM MARKET LOSSES.

2. As you go into it with reasonable expectations, you can be extremely happy when it performs at 11%-12% returns, and when you get early maturities, with gains of 35%-40% you can be ecstatic!

3. With any investment, understand what the risks are and how they can be mitigated and prepared for. With Insurance Settlement Investments, although the exposure is limited and can be planned for and reduced, you'll need to work with your adviser to mitigate it and even eliminate it altogether.

Chapter 9

Get To $1MM With The Millionaire Safety Secret

"You can be young without money, but you can't
be old without it."
- Tennessee Williams

"Money isn't everything...but it ranks right up
there with oxygen."
- Rita Davenport

By now, you have a good understanding of the Millionaire Safety Secret. You know how the numbers work, what's involved and how your money grows. Let's now get into how to use it to create a considerable nest egg. In this chapter you'll see some examples of the parameters that different companies put in place when they consider purchasing a contract from an insured. We'll also cover how you can use insurance settlements with existing money, or money that you're currently going to be putting away for yourself.

It's common to see insurance settlement companies purchase policies that will be available for investment, according to a very specific model and according to a targeted rate of return. This way, investors are able to anticipate very consistent returns. After they run the numbers, if it doesn't meet their targeted rate of return, in most cases the settlement company will turn down the offer to purchase it from the insured, even if it's still a really lucrative buy.

As an investor this gives incredible peace of mind. You know that every policy you've got money in has a specific targeted rate of return and that each policy was purchased with great care and foreknowledge. It allows you to run considerably accurate plans for the future.

It depends on the company, but these targeted rates of return will usually be somewhere between 8%-11%. For one company it might be 9%. For another company, their targeted rate of return might be 11%.

As part of their model, they'll also typically buy policies that fit into their target for life expectancy. Again, for one company it might be 60 months and for another company it might be 84 months. Some might have policies with an average life expectancy of 48 months.

With these numbers you can create a very conservative plan for the future and expect it to perform with targeted accuracy. These numbers allow you to make a stable projection and blueprint. It gives certainty and confidence for how you can expect your money to grow.

Let's take an example for creating $1mm using insurance settlements. In our example, let's say we're working with a company that has a targeted annual rate of return of 10%. What this means is that the majority of their purchased policies will mature with 10% returns, one might mature with 15% and one may mature with 5% returns, but in the end, they will have averaged out and realized their target of 10%.

Also, for our example, let's say the company also purchases their policies with a target of 60 month life expectancies. Again, we don't know when people will die. Some may go in 72 months, and some might go in 48 months, but it will average out at their target of 60 months.

Creating a Predictable Model

With these numbers we can now create a predictable model. On average, it's going to take 60 months for each policy to mature. And on average, these payouts are going to produce 50% returns upon maturity, or the 10% per year target.

Let's jump into the model. If you're 50 years old, your money will grow to $1,012,500 by age 65, if you start today with $300,000.

This is if you don't put any additional money in over the next 15 years. You can imagine what it would be if you continued to add more savings to it on an annual basis!

	Start	300,000 x 50% over 5 years	450,000 x 50% over 5 years	675,000 x 50% over 5 years
Age	50	55	60	65
Secured Nest Egg	$300,000	$450,000	$675,000	$1,012,500

Maybe you don't have $300,000 in liquid funds to start with. Maybe you're getting a late start and only have $25,000, but at this point in your working career, you can also save several thousand dollars for yourself per year. If you want to get to the $1mm mark, you'll need to save just over $3,000 per month. Using insurance settlements, with its protections against loss and no annual percentage fees, you'll have $1,010,625 by the time you're 65 years old.

As you'll see in the following chart, you're saving $3,250 per month for a 15 year period of time. As you continue to save for yourself and your money continues to compound and grow safely inside the insurance settlements, you'll have a considerable nest egg by the time you're ready to retire. But, not only are you helping yourself, you're also helping someone get more for their policy than the insurance company can pay, and the insurance company continues to receive the payment of premiums until the insured passes on.

	Start	$3,250 per month + $25,000 x 50%	$3,250 per month + $232,500 x 50%	$3,250 per month + $543,750 x 50%
Age	50	55	60	65
Secured Nest Egg	$25,000	$232,500	$543,750	$1,010,625

Maybe your situation is a blend of these two examples, or not even close to these two examples. Whatever the case, you can create a model by taking your age, your starting amount, the amount you want to contribute on an annual basis, and then adding the 50% returns every 5 years. Again, this is based on an insurance settlement company that uses a 10% target rate of return and a target life expectancy of 5 years.

These are relatively conservative figures. As we've talked about, high double digit returns are possible and do happen with some regularity. And as a whole, the industry has averaged returns in the teens over last 14 years. But, as you know, it's good to go into it expecting safety against loss, returns that will more than outpace inflation and not being eaten alive by annual percentage fees. If you can accomplish these three things, you'll be on the fast track to a stress-free and abundant future. If you can accomplish these three things, you can do amazing things with your money.

Look at George for example. He's 68 now, but he got started about ten years ago with insurance settlements. He became familiar with them through the help of a long-time friend from college and an adviser to this friend. He started small in 2004, investing $25,000 initially, but added to his account for several years.

He was at a stage in life where he was trying to save as much as he possibly could for his future. As new contracts became available he would put in $5,000-$10,000 here and there a few times per year. He really started to build up a nice portfolio of policies. His wife started encouraging him to look for some safe investments, having lost considerable amounts of money in the stock market on two different occasions. He was also keenly aware and knew that he should be reallocating his money. He would be retiring soon and knew he needed something safe to grow his money.

Five years earlier, they purchased a small cabin with some friends and they were really looking forward to using that a lot more. He was really grateful to have been introduced to this adviser of his friend. He could rest easy knowing his money was safely working for him inside an insurance settlement trust.

After a few years, he had his first payout. It was an early maturity that produced 32% gains! Wow! Now he was really excited. He reinvested this money and continued to let it compound. Starting in his 4th year he started to see more maturities and over the course the next two years, he had received payouts on 8 more. Looking at the numbers, he was averaging 18% per year. In 8 years he received payouts on all but 1 of the initial policies he bought into.

By reinvesting the payouts over the years, he now has money in 90 different policies and is receiving perpetual cash flow at a nice and steady clip. He retired 2 years ago and does just as he and his wife had planned, they spend a lot of time at the cabin with their friends. He knows that rain or shine, hell or high water, he's got an income stream that will keep growing and compounding without any effort of his own doing. His wife is glad too, he used to duck into the home office two or three times per day to check his stock accounts, but now doesn't have to worry about the constant rollercoaster.

Preserving your wealth if you're already a millionaire, or growing your wealth safely to become a cash millionaire can be accomplished with amazing predictability with insurance settlements. There's no other financial tool that does safety, growth, and efficiency quite like it.

Takeaways:

1. Creating $1,000,000 can be accomplished with great accuracy and predictability using the built-in returns of insurance settlement investments.

2. By understanding the model that is used by a particular insurance settlement firm, you can know how many years it will take for your money double and then double again.

Chapter 10

Using The Assistance
Of A Guide

"To accept good advice is but to increase one's own ability."

-Johann Wolfgang von Goethe

A few of my neighbors and I have had to good fortune of working
with the Boy Scout troop here in our area over the last several years
and it amazes me what good and wholesome principles are taught
within the organization. As the scoutmaster, I've had the
opportunity to work with several young men on their progress
toward achieving the coveted rank advancement of Eagle Scout.
It's been an eye opening and enlightening experience as an adviser
to these young men. Some are extremely good at heeding the

counsel that I and other leaders share, but others aren't quite as adept.

On an overnight campout a few years ago, one young man in particular received instruction just like all the other scouts to prepare for a trip up to Big Cottonwood canyon in the Wasatch mountains of northern Utah. The list of suggested gear was laid out in very simple terms and it was just a matter of gathering the gear and making sure it got loaded into the vehicles. The Salt Lake valley in the fall is usually warm, but as you go up in elevation, it can become chilly in a hurry.

We arrived at the camp and got set up, but by nightfall, we noticed that this particular young man didn't bring some of the suggested gear. He had gone for a few hours without complaining, but by the time the sun had gone down and it was time for us to light the campfire and prepare dinner, he was shivering! He could easily see the problem he was in without warm gear. As leaders and with the other scouts, we pooled our resources and provided for him so he could make it through the night comfortably. A month later, on the following campout, I was happy to see that this young man had heeded the advice on the list of gear. He was happy as well.

Seeking Authoritative Counsel

In practical application and actually implementing the insurance settlements strategy, I'm in favor of using a qualified and licensed insurance settlement adviser. It's not the easiest to find an adviser that specializes in insurance settlements, but it's possible and getting easier. It is very worth your time to have a facilitator in this process.

Becoming a client of a good insurance settlement planning specialist not only facilitates the process up front, but it gives you ongoing support with questions, plans, putting in additional funds and what to do with money when there are maturities, whether to take some as a distribution or whether to reinvest and continue to grow as much as you can. It puts you at ease to know someone completely understands your situation, what you're trying to accomplish, what your goals are and your different time frames for distribution.

If putting together a plan for insurance settlement investing is like visiting a foreign country for the first time, then having a good adviser is like having a friend that is a native of that country that will be with you throughout your whole trip, one who speaks the language, that has walked the streets thousands of times and who knows how to navigate the sights like the back of his hand. It gives you confidence so you can relax and completely enjoy your trip.

Plus, with changes happening all the time in our lives, it's smart to have someone with whom to counsel. It's good to have discussions about how those changes can affect our plans and what pivots might be most efficient. It's worth your time to work with someone that's an expert and can hold your hand along the way.

Typically an insurance settlement planning specialist gets paid one time, not an ongoing annual percentage fee. This will allow your money to grow uninhibited by the typical reduction in gains like we've discussed with an IRA or 401k manager. Also, the specialist will normally be paid by the settlement company and not by the investor, allowing all of your funds to immediately participate in the investment.

As mentioned, it's difficult, but not impossible to find an adviser that specializes in insurance settlements. If this book was given to you by an adviser, begin your search by talking with that person. They were probably inclined to pass it along because they know it's crucially important to not lose money due to market crashes and fees, plus have the ability to get good returns to win the inflation battle. It's likely they have an understanding of the insurance settlement marketplace and can help you, or point you in the right direction. Or if you would like a referral to a qualified insurance settlement specialist and other resources, feel free to contact my office at www.MillionaireSafetySecret.com

Takeaways:

1. As you use insurance settlement investments, seek the counsel of a professional who specializes in and knows the industry. A good adviser has walked the path before, will assess your situation, and will know how to help.

2. Use the experience of others to your benefit. Although they're not a dime a dozen, there are many advisers who know the investment extremely well and are willing to help by sharing their expertise.

Part Three

IT'S NOW TIME TO ACT!

Chapter 11

Achieving Financial
Peace Of Mind

"Of course, maintenance of peace of mind, at the maximum extent
possible, would be the greatest success in a human life."
- Chandrababu V.S.

It's common to worry about money. Many people aren't ever able
to stop worrying about it. If it's not about their daily expenses and
costs of living, it's about being able to provide for their children's
or grandchildren's education, or being able to save for their
eventual retirement, or any other myriad of expenses they might
face in their lifetime.

It's also common for many people to have fears about losing their
money if they become disabled or unemployed or through a

downturn in their stock market accounts or through the many fees their paying on their 401k or IRA's. We've been taught for years and years that there are only a handful of ways to grow and accumulate wealth and that those ways are laden with high volatility and extensive risks. The truth is that it doesn't have to be this way. As we've talked about there is a way to completely remove these fears. There's a way to escape these constant anxieties about money.

Yes, this information might conflict with the financial rhetoric that the media, the pop culture financial gurus, the HR department at work, government officials or others have propagated about how to accumulate wealth, but nonetheless, it is the truth. You don't have to use the traditional markets (stock, real estate, precious metals, oil and gas, etc.) that are subject to high volatility, to get good returns.

Blindly following the majority that say "just wait out the crash, the stock market will rebound and return the money you lost", or "you've got to have extensive risk, if you're going to have extensive rewards" will get you exactly what the majority has, which is plenty of worry and concern about their finances.

By using a tool like insurance settlements, with protection against loss, no annual percentage fees, and good returns, you can gain complete financial peace of mind. You can be in a position to have a worry free retirement. Or simply have the option to do so if you choose. You can open yourself up to choices.

*"The significant problems we
face cannot be solved at the
same level of thinking we were
at when we created them."* -
Albert Einstein

One of the problems that we're facing from a financial perspective in America today is that people are placing money they can't afford to lose in vehicles that don't have any protection against loss. In essence, the media has taught us not to have any safe strategies that we can predictably and consistently grow our wealth, but rather to put everything at risk via 401k or IRA contributions that go directly into the stock market. It's fine to use the stock market, real estate market, oil and gas, or the like, with money that you can afford to lose, but not with money you're counting on for the future.

It's fine to invest and go after that huge gain. In fact, with money you can afford to lose, it could be a viable part of your overall financial plan. But consider the peril that's involved by having *all* your money in accounts that are subject to loss.

So far, as we've discussed the principles in this book, hopefully you've started think about your money from a different angle. It is absolutely possible to have the peace of mind that comes with a predictable, simple and consistent financial strategy that will serve your needs now and for decades to come. Obviously this isn't a strategy to get wealthy overnight. By no means am I saying you can "get rich quick" with insurance settlements, but you absolutely can get rich or stay rich with it. As with anything else in life, it just take a bit of patience and persistence.

Being Introduced to Something New

Over the years I've grown to love Apple computers. Their sleek design and easy-to-use software is fun and functional. I'll admit, I wasn't the first to adopt the Mac as a personal computer. Maybe I had just been in a personal computing cave, but it actually took me a while to even realize there were other options than just the traditional PC. I didn't know what I didn't know. I had no idea what I was missing.

After being introduced to Apple computers and gadgets and then getting some more information and education on them I realized something incredible, that for a long time, I had been completely oblivious to. It's not because I was trying to hide from different options, or that I wasn't looking for other options because I knew steadfastly that the PC was a better computer, it was simply the fact that it took me a while to be introduced to another option with Apple computers. It was simply a lack of education on my part.

Once I got information and education on Apple and started to use one myself, I was opened up to a "whole new personal computing world" per se. So it is with anything in life. We don't know what we don't know.

Once we figure something out, get new information or new knowledge, our life can change for the better. I think Albert

Einstein's definition of insanity is a good one. It's crazy to keep doing the same thing over and over again, but expecting different results each time.

I'll also admit, that I do still use a PC as well, but for different things. The two computers do separate things well. Because I'm educated on how to use both computers, I can use either one for the objective I'm trying to accomplish. Similarly, like I mentioned, I don't think it's a terrible idea to have money in the stock market with the objective to go after a big gain, just use money that you're not depending on for the future and understand that it can be completely lost.

You don't have to spend your entire life worrying about whether or not your nest egg will be there when you need it. Or if it will be enough to last your entire life. It's possible to get yourself on a financial path that is different from what you're on now. It's possible for you to achieve a high level of control, security, and freedom with your money that you may not have thought was achievable. It just takes the knowledge, a bit of time and some effort in the right direction.

Takeaways:

1. You can experience a high degree of financial peace of mind when you've removed money from vehicles that have high risk and volatility, and yet still have the ability to get very good rates of return consistently and predictably.

2. Financial peace of mind comes from not having to worry about whether your money will be there when you need it. It comes from knowing that you're getting the returns you need in order to maintain your lifestyle as long as you live.

Chapter 12

The Life You've Dreamed Of

"We must learn to help those who deserve it, not just those who
need it. Life responds to deserve, not need."
- Jim Rohn

"There are three ingredients in the good life: learning,
earning and yearning."
- Christopher Morley

"All our dreams can come true, if we have the courage
to pursue them."
- Walt Disney

The quote by Jim Rohn at the beginning of this chapter really has
some resonance. Life truly does respond to deserve, and by taking
responsibility for your own financial future you become deserving
of the best outcomes possible. You deserve the best financial
future you can create.

You've worked hard for your entire life. You've taken care of
business, you've likely raised a family or are in the process of

94

raising a family and added value to your community. You've put in the time and made the sacrifices. You deserve a good lifestyle. One that will allow you complete freedom and peace of mind. One where you don't have to worry about whether or not you're going to have enough money or have to come out of retirement and go back into the workforce.

Imagine you've taken the steps to secure your financial house. You've done all the necessary things to ensure you won't lose money in a market crash. You're set up to keep the lion's share of your earnings by not having any annual percentage fees to rob you of 60% of your total nest egg. You're in a vehicle that abundantly outpaces inflation, giving you the freedom to continue a lifestyle you're accustomed to and not having to worry about going back to work in the later years of life.

Just imagine for a moment... you've secured a good portion of your nest egg and gotten it out of the market. You've sequestered it into an investment where you don't have to worry about the volatility of the market.

You no longer have to be concerned about world events affecting your nest egg. Worrying about whether North Korea will sporadically attack, or if there will be an earthquake and tsunami that hits Japan that causes the market to plummet, or whether the Middle East will erupt, or some other global upheaval that affects the fragile mindset of emotional investors, or frankly, any other host of things that can affect whether or not you'll be able to count on your nest egg to be there when you need it most.

Imagine all of those factors are off the table. Your money is in a secure place with predictable, stable and consistent growth. It might not grow by 30% every single year, but at least it won't lose 52% in a matter of 18 months like we saw just a few years ago in 2008.

Imagine the joy of being able to do what you've always wanted to do. This is what you deserve. After so many years of hard work, struggle, toil, sacrifice, and diligence, this is truly what you're entitled to, a safe path to maintaining and growing your wealth.

How does it feel at that point? I'm sure it feels pretty good. I imagine it feels exhilarating to know you've beaten the financial pitfalls that beset so many Americans. That you can go to sleep at night without the stress and worry of whether or not you'll have enough money when you need it. I imagine a weight has been lifted off your shoulders, knowing you've removed the volatility from your plans and gotten on board a safety locomotive, powering you through to your destination.

With insurance settlements there's really more than one return on investment. Yes, the monetary increase is good, but there are also returns that can't easily be measured in dollars and cents. There's a return that comes in the form of peace of mind, one that comes in the form of predictability, another one that comes in the form of time freedom, and yet another that comes in efficiency and simplicity.

Imagine the peace of mind that will come the morning after you've moved your money. You can now really start to think about what you're going to do with your retirement years. You're not bogged down by uncertainty. You now have more freedom and more control. You can now really start to enjoy yourself.

At the point where this happens, where you've secured yourself into a vehicle in which you've got safety, incredible gains, and extremely low fees, you can now focus on helping others or giving back in some way. This is where it gets really fun. This is where you can really have fulfillment in your life.

I'm not saying you need to wait until you're completely and totally financially independent, where you'll never need to worry about money again, to start helping others. I'm saying you can do a lot more for others, when you're not having to be concerned about your own financial house. At this point, you can really establish a legacy of your choosing.

Takeaways:

1. Position yourself to enjoy what is deservedly yours. Remove financial worry from your life and gain the peace of mind that comes with not having to worry about losing money.

2. Take action toward this lifestyle today by reaching out to an insurance settlement investment specialist, someone who can help you get secured from the volatility of the market.

Afterword

Give Without End

"What do we live for, if it is not to make life less difficult
for each other?"

- George Eliot

"Giving should be entered into in just the same way as investing.
Giving is investing."

- John D. Rockefeller

I don't know if there's any better feeling than to walk away from something, knowing you've made a positive impact for the benefit of someone else. To know you've left your mark, and that you've helped someone in their journey, is extremely satisfying and fulfilling. I'm sure you've seen this in your own life.

As you've noticed in this book, I'm a huge fan of simplicity. I think much can be gained by taking something complex, complicated and convoluted and making it simple. It's something that brings me joy.

I was taught this lesson at a young age. After high school, I had the opportunity to spend a significant amount of time in a developing country teaching and doing service. I learned many life lessons by working with hundreds and hundreds of indigenous people over the span of 22 months. One of the lessons I'd like to share here is the happiness that comes from giving in simple ways.

In my travels among the people I was serving, I would often be invited in to share a meal. For the first few months, as a first world American, I was shocked at the living conditions of this country. Shanty dwellings, dirt floors, and no doors in many homes was very common.

As they shared and gave of their meal with me, I was constantly amazed at the look on their face as I would take the first few bites of whatever it was we were eating. It was a look of pure happiness and joy. They would get excited just by seeing me eat and enjoy what they shared.

It wasn't just occasionally or in a few homes that I noticed this. In just about every home I had the opportunity to be in and share a meal, they were always happy to see me eating and enjoying what they had given me. I'm convinced they know something that people in many fully developed countries don't know, or maybe they know, but often forget; that a fullness of happiness can come by simply giving.

A Legacy of Shared Money is Good

With an investment like Insurance Settlements where you're not going to lose principal or earnings and where you can count on sizeable returns year after year, you can be in a position to be very generous with money. Giving might just be the most satisfying and fulfilling thing you will ever do with your money. You might get

101

tired of your hobbies, or buying the newest and shiniest things. You might have traveled so much that you're ready to stay in one spot for a while. But giving, and seeing the happiness and joy that can come to another when you share and serve rarely gets old.

Just about every single mentally, emotionally, and spiritually prosperous person I've known gets a kick out of giving abundantly. We see examples of this all over the place. But you have to be in a position to be able to derive joy and happiness from this. If you're worried about how you're going to stretch your fixed income just to cover your bills, giving of your money to another will create stress, rather than peace, joy and happiness.

But if you think about it, have you ever met an extremely generous person that's unhappy? I think it's safe to say that generosity with money can lead to genuine happiness. It's almost as if generosity is a switch that once flipped, turns on a flow of good things.

When Andrew Carnegie was 13 years old, he and his family arrived in America from Scotland. He started working immediately in a cotton mill and moved quickly up through the ranks. He worked for the major railroad companies of the day and brought huge amounts of value wherever he was planted.

In 1865, he started his own company that later became the Carnegie Steel Company. At age 65 he sold it to J.P. Morgan for $480 million and for the rest of his life he gave the majority of his wealth away.

In large part, it's because of Andrew Carnegie that we have the U.S. public library system. He believed in the education of the working class and was passionate about its cause. It's estimated that he gave away close to $400 million before the end of his life. When he died, they found a page in one of his writings that outlined one of his major life goals: to spend the first half of his life accumulating as much wealth as possible and the last half of his life giving it all away. He did just that!

Let's delve into this some more and explore it from another angle as well. This book is about removing your money from vehicles that have extreme volatility and high costs and replacing them with a consistent and stable vehicle so you can safely and abundantly grow your nest egg.

At its core, this book is about safety with money. How does generosity apply to safety? How am I being safe with my money, if I'm giving it away? It's my opinion that giving money away to causes you're passionate about is one of the safest investments you can possibly make. It's an investment for the future that will make its way around.

It's a law of life that we reap what we sow. It's also a law that we reap in larger proportions of that which we sow. We sow little seeds and reap plentiful crops. Giving, even just a little, makes an investment that pays bountiful dividends for the rest of our lives.

If you reap plentiful and bounteous crops by sowing just a little, think of the magnitude and scale you'll receive by sowing much. Can there be a safer investment for your future?

A Legacy of Shared Time is Better

It may not have been with money that you've helped someone substantially, maybe it was something even more valuable than money, maybe it was your time that you gave to someone.

This is far and away our most valuable resource. We can always make more money, but we can't always make more time. It is our

103

most scarce resource, there's a finite amount of it that we all have. It's something we just cannot get some more of. So if time is what you've given someone, to benefit their life, I applaud that heartedly.

We all have to provide for our own needs, it's the reality of life. If we don't use our time wisely, we know the consequences. As we've discussed in this book, we know we have to get certain things done to take care of ourselves first. But once those things are handled and taken care, you'll experience wealth freedom as well as time freedom.

This is where you can really make a difference. By giving of your time, you can leverage the impact for good you can make in someone's life. With all the knowledge, skill, talent, and faculties you've developed over the course of your life, you've become an extremely valuable resource for the world. How fulfilling it is to share that with others. This can be done in large capacity with the time freedom that will come by not having to worry about your investments.

Think of the countless organizations that can use help in promoting and maintaining activism in good causes. Think of the family members, friends, co-workers, neighbors, and people in the community that can be benefitted by your talents. By giving of your time to these organizations and people, you can be filled to the brim of excitement and adventure. True fulfillment comes from actively serving and helping others. This is one of the keys to a robust, prosperous and confident life.

It's fascinating to see what benefits come to those that devote their time to others through service. By being able to give your time to others, you inherently increase your own health and happiness.

So many centenarians have attributed their longevity to actively being engaged in serving and helping others. You may not want to live until age 100, but if you didn't have to worry about your investments and having enough money, and continued to be able to contribute in meaningful ways, it might change your mind.

By arranging your investments in such a way that you don't have to worry about the flowing income, you can dedicate the majority of your time to something that has purpose and meaning for you. This is what brings true happiness, spending time where it counts for you. This is what will bring positivity and fervor into your life. This is what will allow you to be an inspiration to those you care about.

The benefits that will come to you because of how you dedicate your time and service to others will be unmatched by any other achievements you may have had in your life. Being in a position to give of your time to causes and people you care about will be an infinite and abundant fountain of youth. This is a key to keeping your life full, meaningful and spirited.

A Legacy of Shared Knowledge is Best

The knowledge you give truly has the ability to go on perpetually. This is why it's one of my last points of discussion. This is one of the most important things you can give your heirs, posterity, community, friends, colleagues, neighbors, associates, and all others you interact with in some way.

This is what you'll truly be known for. What did you use your life to become? It's my belief that our knowledge is the only thing we'll take with us as we go on to the greener pastures of the next life.

It's truly the only thing that will have an endless and recurring impact after we're gone. The knowledge we share with others, will inherently be shared with those of future and subsequent generations, and so on and so on, forever. Though it might be modified or changed to meet the needs of current conditions, a piece of what is passed on can come from the legacy of knowledge we pass on.

With the peace of mind, abundant lifestyle and the ability to live a life of giving that financial independence can bring, how important it is to share these principles with others. How important to instill in your children and grandchildren the principle that they don't have to risk their life savings to be able to get good returns. Likely being younger, imagine the savings they can realize over the course of their lives by not having to pay an annual percentage fee to an IRA or 401k manager. Making sure your family has the knowledge they need in order to deal with inflation, have rock solid gains and build on a sure financial foundation is one of the most culminating gifts you can give them. By sharing that with them, you can leave a legacy that will continue on long after you're gone.

Takeaways:

1. Position yourself to be able to give abundantly. Experience the joy, happiness, peace and exhilaration that comes from seeing the excitement of someone you've just shared with.

2. Giving of your money is good. Giving of your time is better. Giving of your knowledge is best. Take the necessary steps now to be able to leave a legacy of knowledge, financial freedom and abundance for future generations.

Additional Resources

For a free, personalized insurance settlement toolkit, or for a referral to a qualified insurance settlement specialist, feel free to contact my office at: www.MillionaireSafetySecret.com

CONTACT

If you'd like to work personally with Brian or you're looking for a financial strategist or planning expert, feel free to contact our office by visiting:

www.MillionaireSafetySecret.com

Brian is licensed and operates his business in over 30 states. He has trained hundreds of advisers one-on-one and currently serves as mentor to an elite group of safe money advisers from across the nation. He is the founder of the Millionaire Safety Group located in South Jordan, Utah. As of 2014, he is accepting new clients and working one-on-one with individuals. Currently, in order to spend the adequate and appropriate time for each client's unique situation, he only takes on 10 new clients per month. But, whatever your situation, don't hesitate to inquire at the website above and request a free, personalized insurance settlement toolkit. It will be promptly sent to you via USPS mail. If you'd like to work with Brian personally, it may be necessary to put your name on the notification list. Currently the wait time is 2-4 weeks. But additional tools, information and resources will be sent in the interim and the notification list is continually updated with the most recent news and information. Appointments are scheduled and taken on a first come, first served basis. If immediate assistance is required, a referral can be given to a qualified Millionaire Safety Group specialist.

ABOUT THE AUTHOR

Brian Lund works with individuals, families, corporate executives, professionals and business owners in developing and taking action on personalized and custom financial strategies. He mentors advisers in the financial services industry to do the same. Brian considers himself a teacher at heart. His approach is to educate and empower his clients to secure their financial future, making it possible to enjoy a worry-free retirement and a wide variety of options with their finances. He speaks at a multitude of conferences and events each year. To inquire about having him speak at your event please visit: www.MillionaireSafetySecret.com

Brian is very involved with his family, church, and community. He enjoys working with the Boy Scouts of America, camping, hiking, and spending time with his wife and three children. He currently resides in South Jordan, Utah.